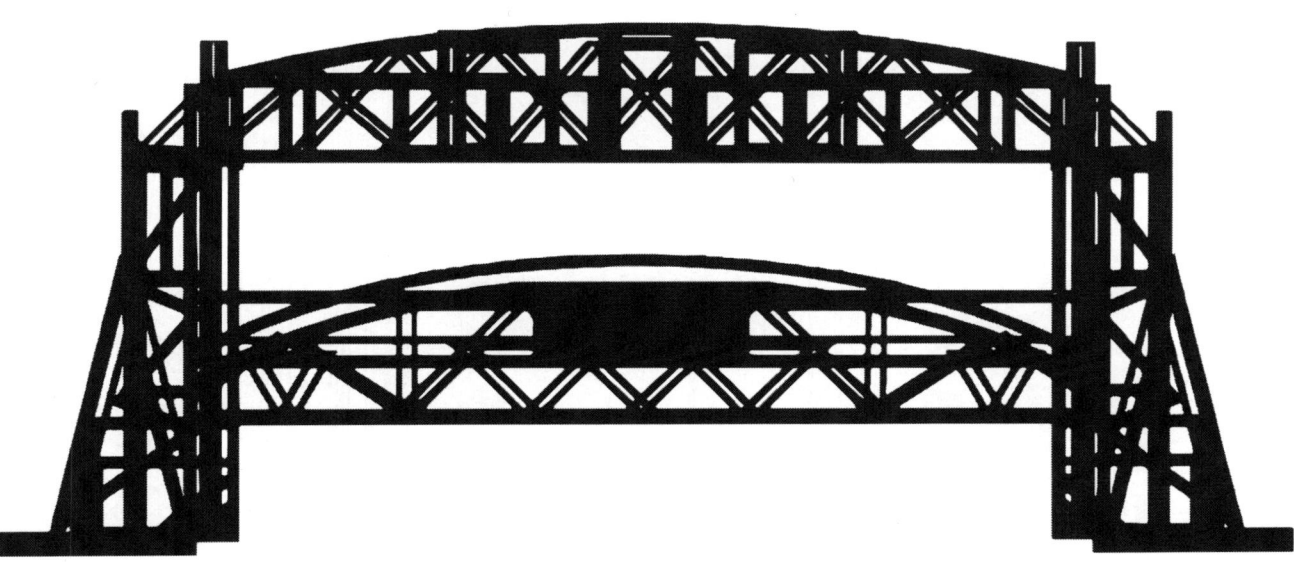

CAN YOU UNSCRAMBLE THE LETTERS TO NAME THE GREAT LAKES?

OEIRRPUS

_ _ _ _ _ _ _ _

INMAHIGC

_ _ _ _ _ _ _ _

URONH

_ _ _ _ _

IREE

_ _ _ _

ROTINAO

_ _ _ _ _ _ _

TIC TAC TOE

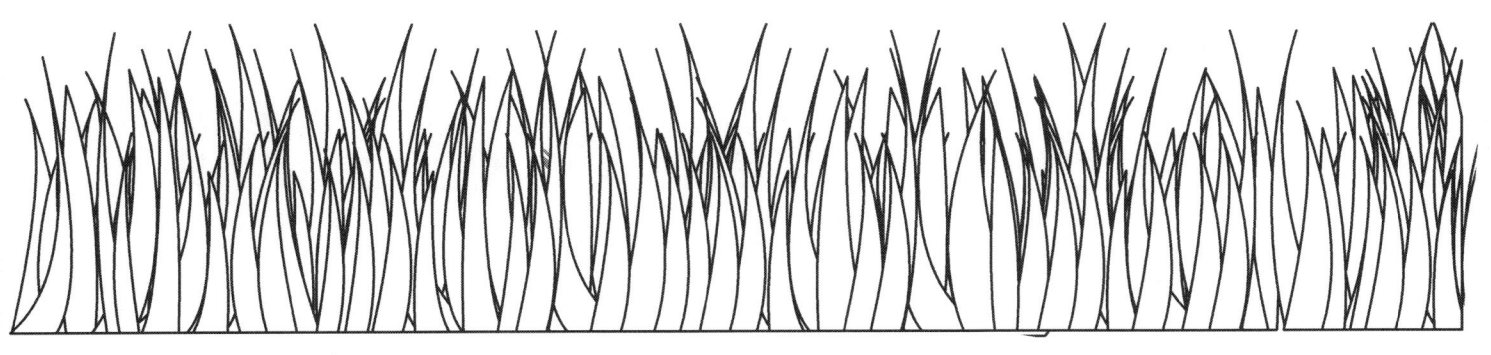

CONNECT THE DOTS

CAUGHT FISH

Player 1 thinks of a word or a short phrase.

Player 2 tries to figure out what the phrase is by guessing letters.

If player 2 guesses a correct letter, fill in the letter on the blank spaces and cross it out.

If player 2 guesses a wrong letter, the fish is drawn, one part at a time for each wrong letter.

Player 1 wins if the fish is drawn in. Player 2 wins if they guess the phrase or all the letters before all the fish parts are drawn.

Line, body, head, 4 fins, eye, and mouth.
See below for an example.

A B C D E F G H I J K L M

N O P Q R S T U V W X Y Z

Dots and Boxes

This is a two-player game. Each player needs a different color pen.

Players take turns joining two dots by a line (horizontally or vertically adjacent). The player that completes the fourth side of a box colors that box in and plays again. The game ends when all boxes have been colored. The player who has the most boxes colored wins the game.

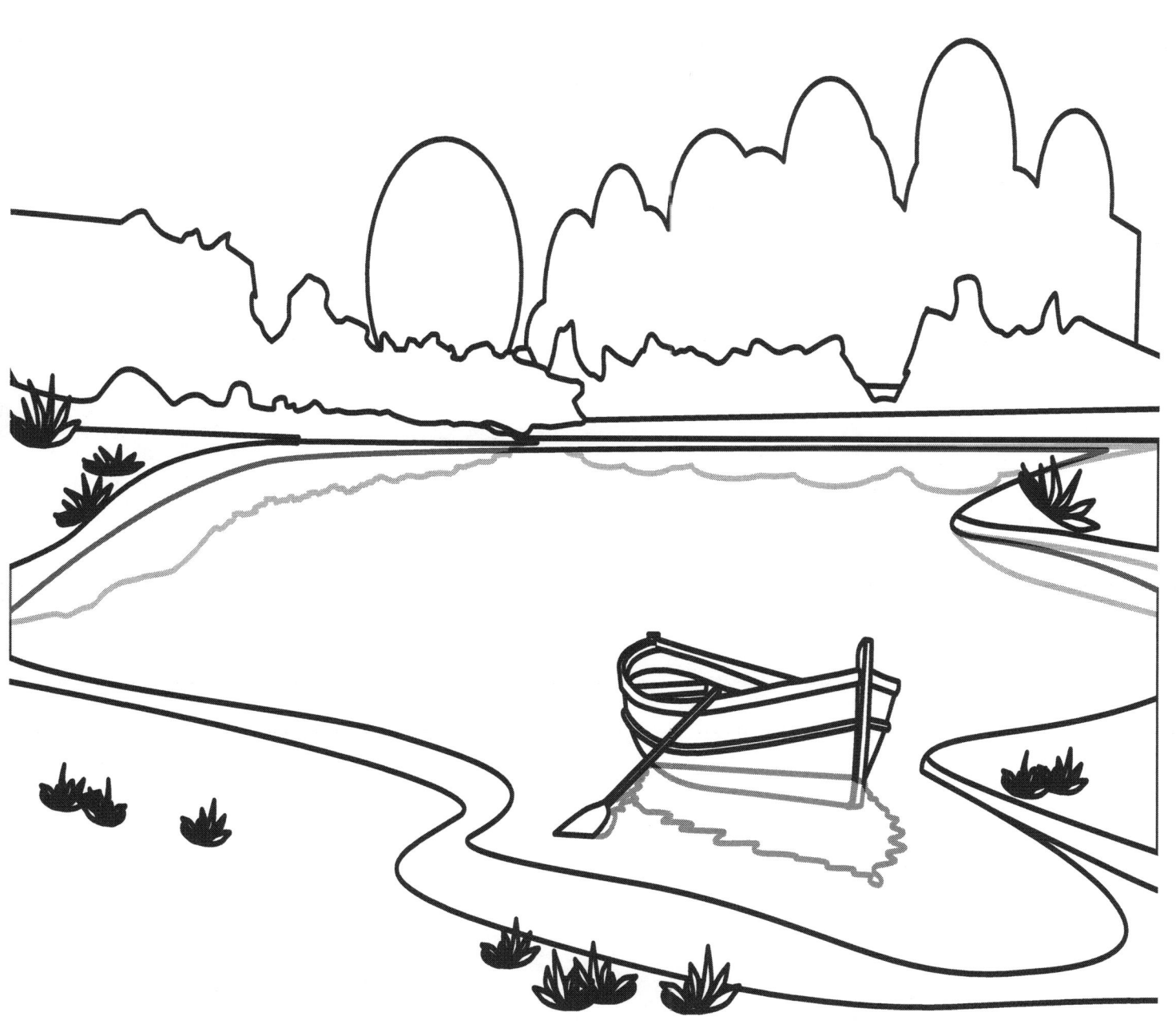

SUDOKU #1

Each row, column, and box needs the numbers
1 through 6 to complete the puzzle.

		5	4	2	
2	1				
1		6		3	
	5	3			
		1	2		
		2	1	5	6

CONNECT THE DOTS

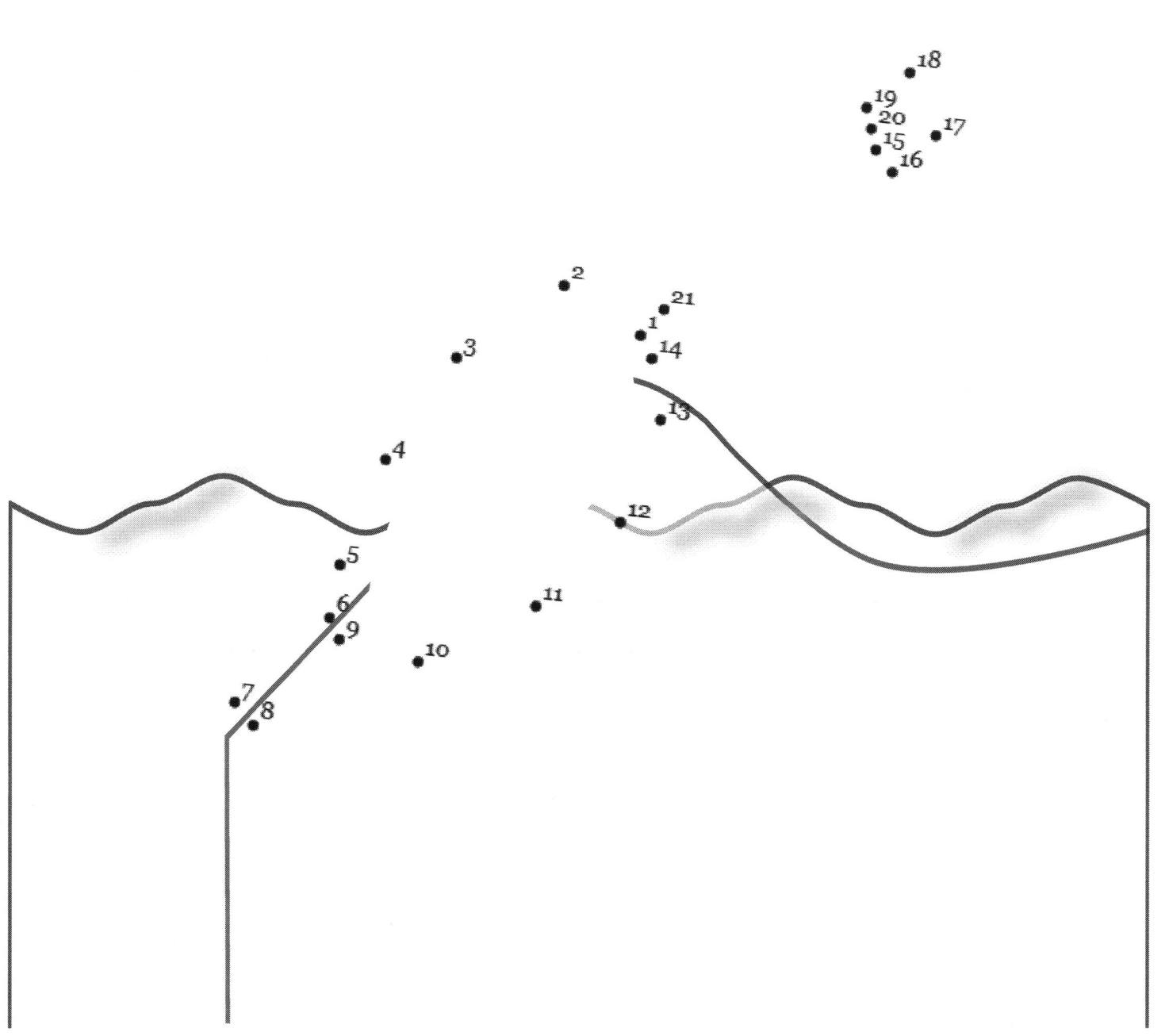

FISHING STORY

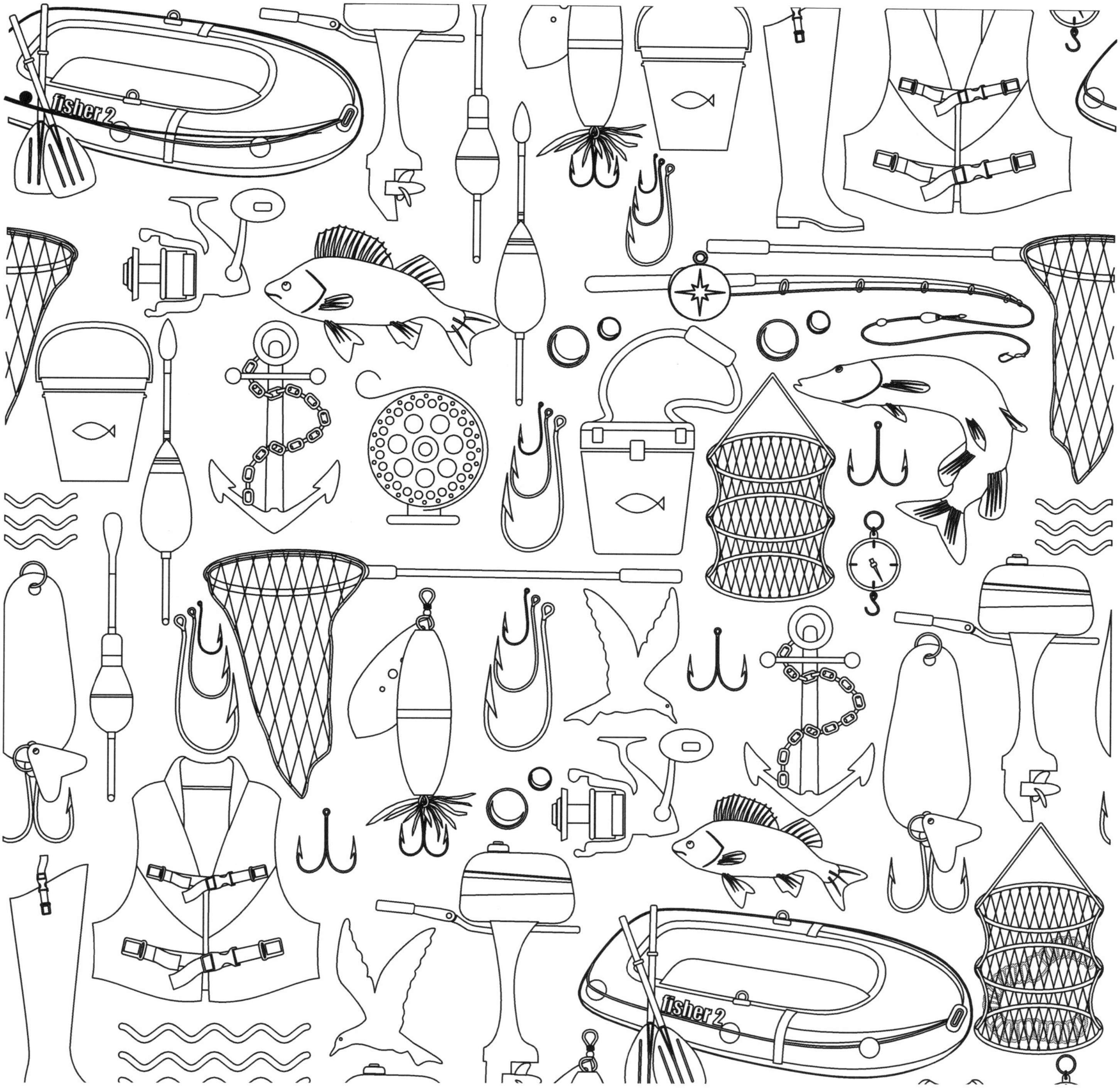

Can you find these hidden objects?

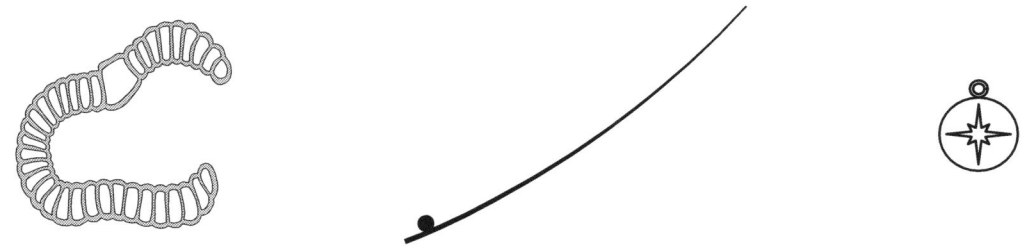

SUDOKU #2

Each row, column, and box needs the numbers
1 through 6 to complete the puzzle.

		1	4		
4					1
5			2	1	6
		6	3		5
1		4		2	3
	5		1		4

CONNECT THE DOTS

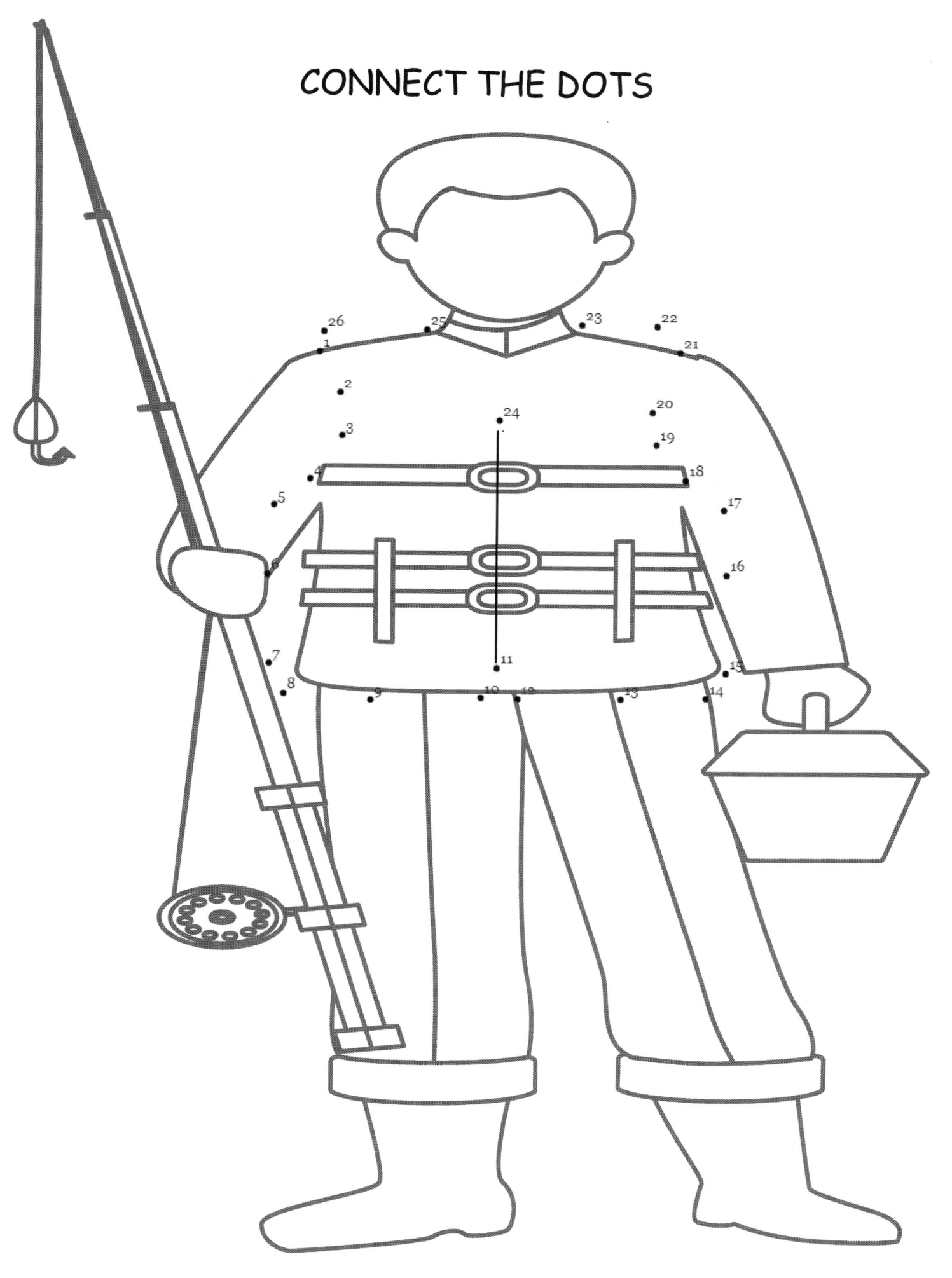

FRESHWATER FISH
CROSSWORD PUZZLE

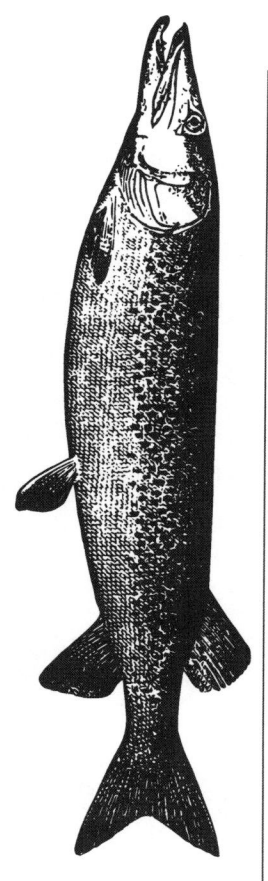

```
S  N  L  N  O  M  L  A  S  H
V  S  O  L  S  T  R  O  U  T
C  V  A  E  I  U  Q  T  N  C
S  R  X  B  G  G  C  H  V  N
U  R  A  G  B  R  E  K  O  N
N  F  C  P  E  D  U  U  E  R
F  C  F  V  P  A  L  T  L  R
I  C  A  T  F  I  S  H  S  B
S  Y  M  V  D  P  E  R  C  H
H  U  X  N  E  I  K  S  U  M
```

BASS	BLUEGILL
CATFISH	CRAPPIE
GAR	MUSKIE
PERCH	SALMON
STURGEON	SUCKER
SUNFISH	TROUT

Ice Fishing

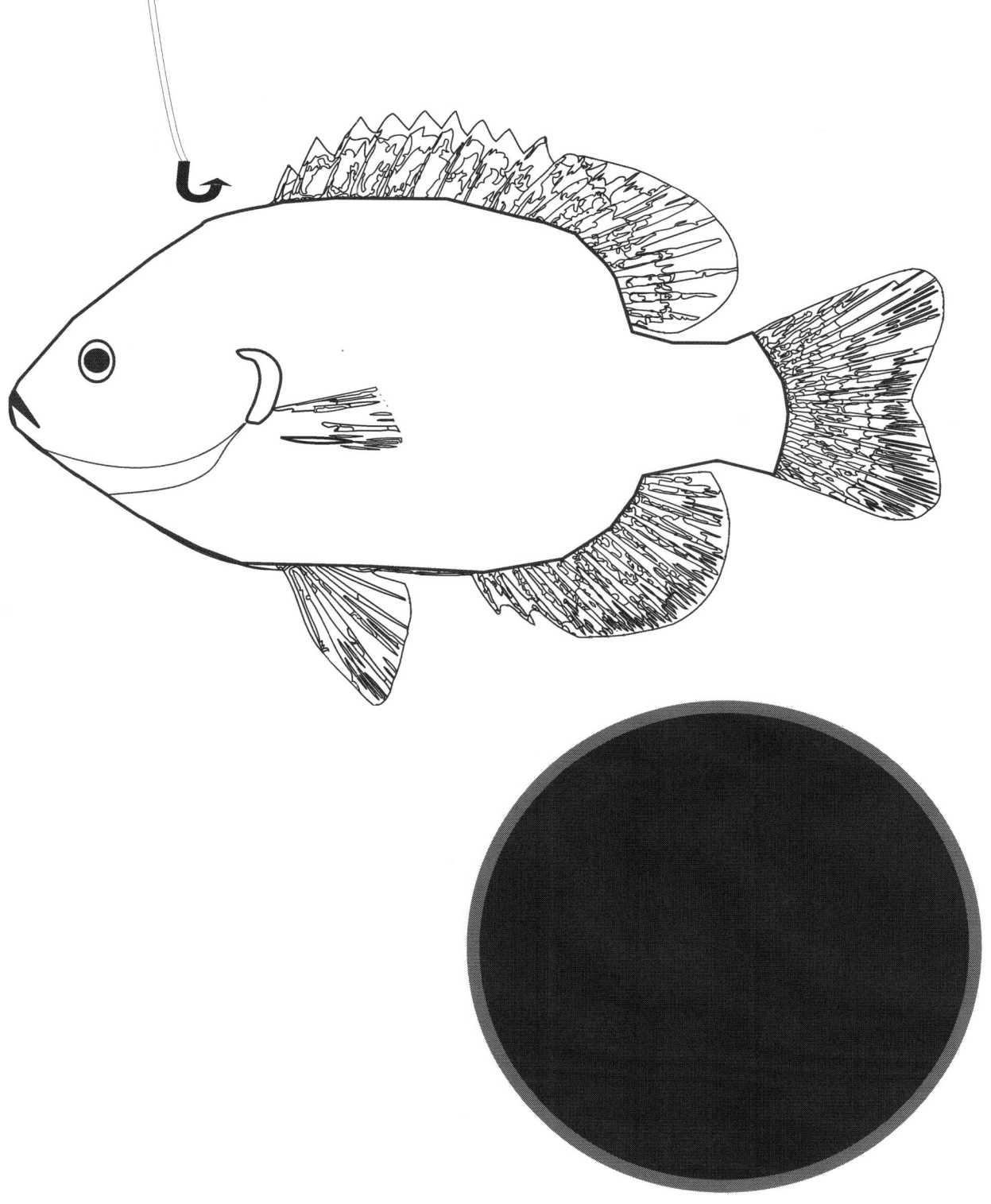

SUDOKU #3

Each row, column, and box needs the numbers
1 through 9 to complete the puzzle.

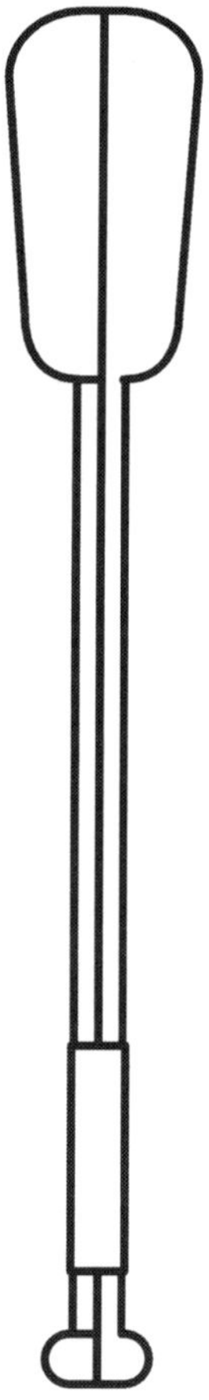

6		3	8		9		2	5
2	8		5					1
9	5		4	2	3	6		7
1			2			7	4	
4			3		6			
8	6			7				
						5		
7	4	8					9	2
					1		6	4

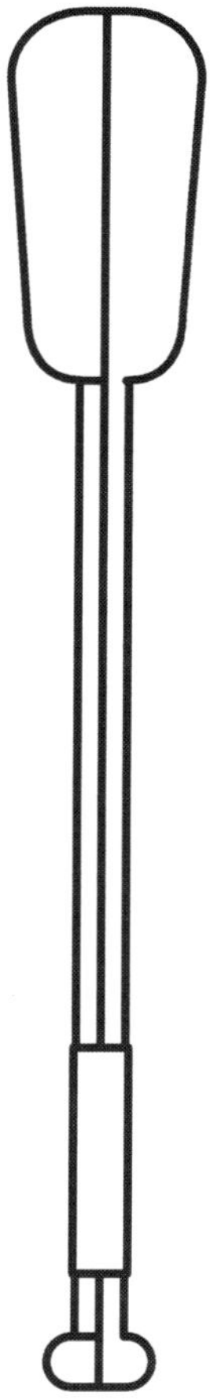

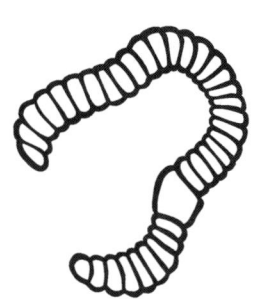 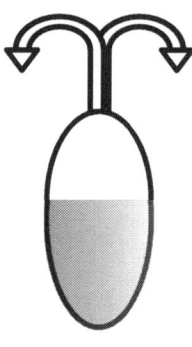  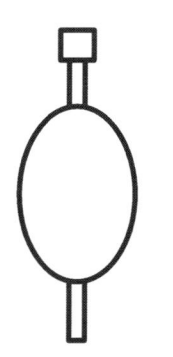 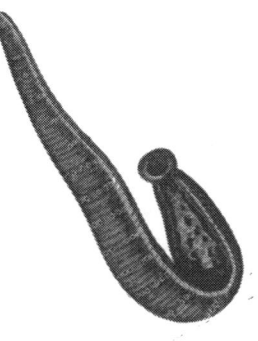

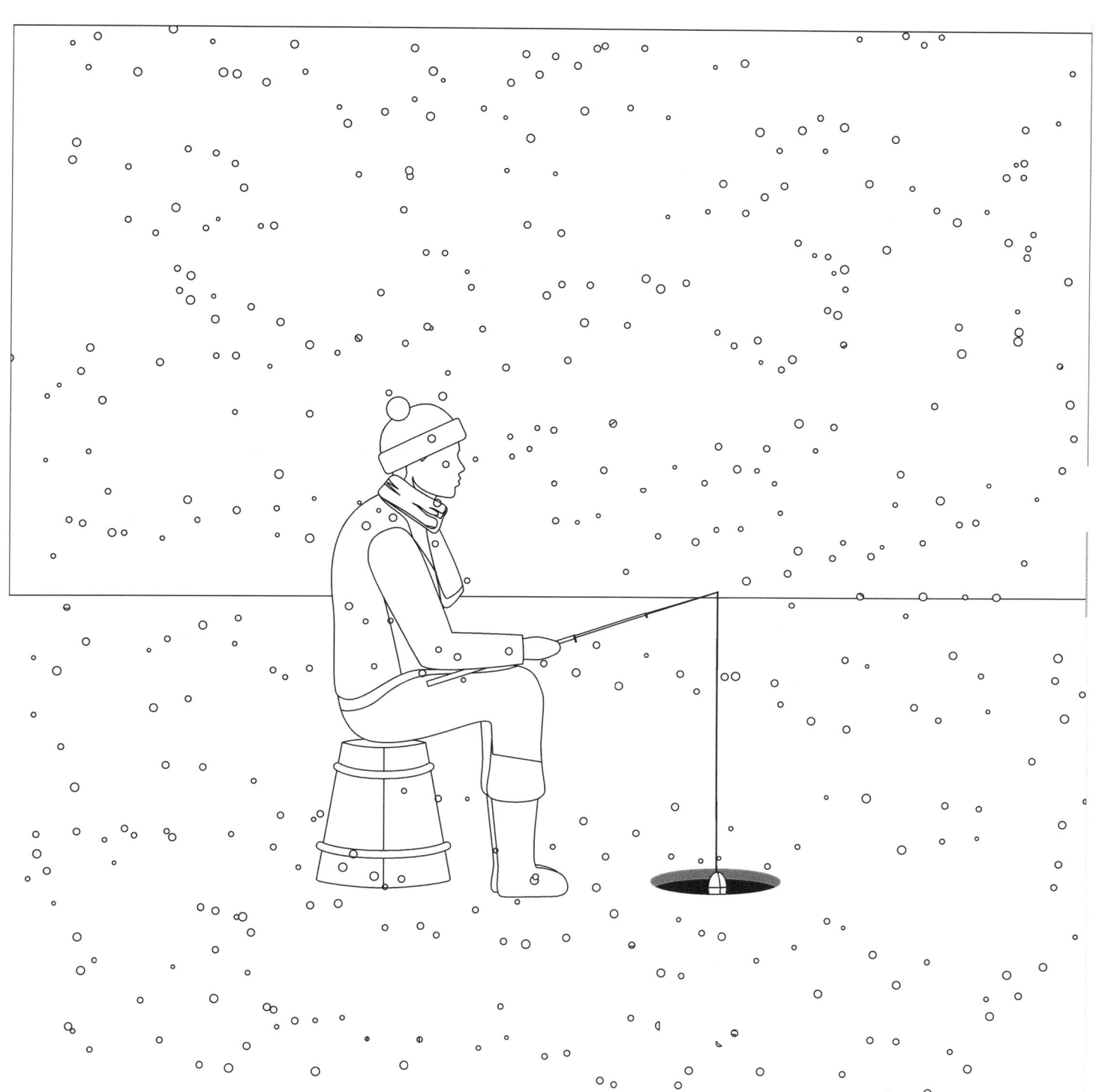

Check Your Answers

GREAT LAKES
SCRAMBLE
ANSWERS

OEIRRPUS	SUPERIOR
INMAHIGC	MICHIGAN
URONH	HURON
IREE	ERIE
ROTINAO	ONTARIO

FRESHWATER FISH
CROSSWORD PUZZLE
ANSWERS

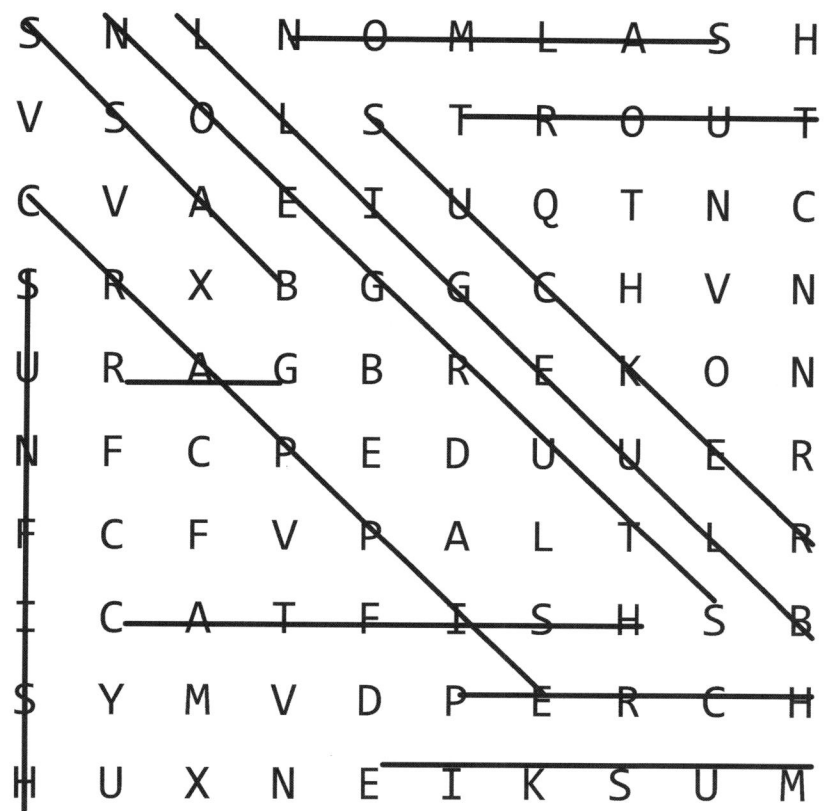

BASS	BLUEGILL
CATFISH	CRAPPIE
GAR	MUSKIE
PERCH	SALMON
STURGEON	SUCKER
SUNFISH	TROUT

SUDOKU #1 & 2
ANSWERS

6	3	5	4	2	1
2	1	4	3	6	5
1	2	6	5	3	4
4	5	3	6	1	2
5	6	1	2	4	3
3	4	2	1	5	6

6	3	1	4	5	2
4	2	5	6	3	1
5	4	3	2	1	6
2	1	6	3	4	5
1	6	4	5	2	3
3	5	2	1	6	4

SUDOKU #3
ANSWERS

6	7	3	8	1	9	4	2	5
2	8	4	5	6	7	9	3	1
9	5	1	4	2	3	6	8	7
1	3	5	2	9	8	7	4	6
4	2	7	3	5	6	8	1	9
8	6	9	1	7	4	2	5	3
3	1	6	9	4	2	5	7	8
7	4	8	6	3	5	1	9	2
5	9	2	7	8	1	3	6	4

Just a Note:

I hope you enjoyed this book!

Thank you so much for your purchase!

If you liked this book, please consider looking at some of my other activity books.

I would love to see a review or any feedback that you may have.

However, If you prefer to contact me personally with suggestions please email me at healthyhappyfarm@gmail.com or visit me at

https://healthyhappyfarm.com

Sincerely,

Amy